Prayer & the Redwood Seed

OTHER BOOKS
BY MORTON KELSEY

PRAYER & THE REDWOOD SEED

MORTON T. KELSEY

E L E M E N T

Rockport, Massachusetts ● Shaftesbury, Dorset

© 1991 Morton T. Kelsey
Published in the U.S.A. in 1991 by
Element, Inc.
42 Broadway, Rockport, MA 01966

Published in Great Britain in 1991 by
Element Books Limited
Longmead, Shaftesbury, Dorset

Printed in the United States of America.

Interior Design: E. Dorian Sweet

Cover Design: Barbara McGavin

Cover Photograph: Breck Kent/Oxford Scientific Films

Library of Congress Cataloging-in-Publication Data
Kelsey, Morton T.
  Prayer & the redwood seed: a meditation on the tree of life/
Morton T. Kelsey.
    1. Tree of life—Meditations.   I. Title.   II. Title: Prayer and
the redwood seed.
BV4832.2.K417   1991
242—dc20   91–30108

ISBN 1–85230–264–X

CONTENTS

To Holly Ashleen Kelsey, my youngest grandchild.

PREFACE

I live in a very special place, among the redwoods on the northern coast of California. Our little house and cabin appear doll-like, dwarfed by these towering second growth trees. The incredible persistence, age and size of these monarchs of the forest still strike me with amazement and wonder when I meditate upon these companions whose land I share. At times they seem almost presences as I walk among them.

Redwoods are the largest and tallest living creatures. The trees among which I live sometimes reach three hundred and sixty feet to sweep the sun's rays from the sky. They are babies at a hundred years, adolescent at five hundred and mature around a thousand years of age. The rings on fallen trees reveal that some of them have lived twenty-five hundred years.

The Sierra cousins of the coast sequoia are so immense
that I had forgotten their size until a recent visit to them. The
General Sherman tree is over thirty-five feet in diameter at
the base and is still fourteen feet in diameter one hundred
and eighty feet above the ground. Its largest branch is nearly
seven feet through the center. And the tree is still growing
and adding each year a volume of wood equivalent to a tree
fifty feet high and a foot at its base. It has lived some three
thousand years. One needs to stand beneath them, ant-like,
to grasp their meaning.

Both the giant redwoods and their coastal relatives have
withstood earthquake, fire, and flood. Their fire-resistant
bark saves the trees from the fire that cleans the grounds of
undergrowth and even aids the germination of seeds falling
from the giant trees.

These trees are found in fossils over a hundred and fifty
million years of age. There were great groves of redwoods
through which the dinosaurs lumbered, stopping to rest in
their shade.

The great reptiles are all extinct, but the redwoods con-
tinued to flourish until they covered most of the northern
hemisphere from the Pacific coast of North America, through
Europe to the coast of China. They now remain as native
trees in only three places: along the coast and in the high
mountains of California, and also in a remote valley of
mountainous China.

The most astounding fact of all is that these trees spring
from seeds so tiny that it takes three to six thousand of them
to weigh an ounce. Great majestic trees rise from these tiny
embryos and sweep the sky to embrace and capture the sunlight. We human beings have microscopic beginnings within

a woman's womb and then are born and grow. We search out the great world around us and wander over its vast surface. And then if we find this world does not satisfy our deepest seeking, we find we can enter another domain to which we also belong. We can be transformed, divinized and share in the kingdom of heaven and of God where our growth is infinite. Our potential exceeds even that of the redwood seed.

SEED

— 1 —

Awed and quiet within a grove of giant redwoods, I pause
reflecting.
In my hand I hold a tiny seed, a redwood seed.
It lies inert upon my wrinkled palm.
Several thousand do not weigh an ounce.
A gust of wind could carry it away.
My fingernail could rip it open and destroy
its life.
So many thousands fall to the ground and perish.
They fall upon the rocky soil and do not
germinate.
They spring up and are devoured by hungry
forest creatures.
They are so fragile and powerless.

I wonder how these seeds can give birth
   to a living cathedral like this in which I stand.
      Gigantic buttresses of wood and bark
      support great tapering columns arching
      overhead,
      filtering a stream of soft light
      upon carpets of ferns and fallen twigs.
I feel as tiny as the seed I hold.

   Wandering through the mountains on the foggy
California coast
      I come upon the giant stumps of fallen redwoods
      standing like sentinels among the smaller trees.
      I also find the stubs of younger trees, all that
   is left
      when saw and ax have done their work.
Ancient Titans so thoughtlessly cut down, younger trees-
      destroyed, before maturity.
   And then I see
   a ring of great trees has risen
      from the roots of the colossal stump.
         And springing up from hidden life, remains
         of younger trees,
         are living shoots, which will become huge
   trees in time.
            These descendants of younger trees cut down,
            will someday produce another ring of giants.

I gaze upon that tiny seed and the charred and splin-
tered ruins
    of once noble trees.
And then I look up into the magnificent redwoods
surrounding me,
    laughing and dancing in the breeze.
How grand and powerful they are
    And yet they issued from a small grain of life
    like that lying on my hand
      or else they sprang from death and
      devastation.
  I am amazed, awed and filled with wonder.
    I watch the dying sun still blazing on
their crests
    after it has dropped below the horizon and my
    sight.

These tallest of living creatures have an ancient lineage,
and some of the great trees have lived for many centuries.
Eons pass and still they thrive and grow.
  Some of them were living in Caesar's time.
  The roots reach out, a fishnet cast into the earth,
  Immense trunks stretch up, point to the sky,
    throwing another net of branches, twigs and
    needles,
    into the invisible nutrients of air
    and presenting a mighty crown of greenery, an
    offering
    to the sun from which it draws its very life.

Great storms sweep in from raging seas.
  The towering columns sway back and forth,
    the rain falls, an intricate web of rootlets
      drinks in the riches of the soil.
  The same living net holds the earth around it like a
cloak;
    even torrential floods do not wash the earth
    away.
  Lightning flashes and strikes a mammoth tree.
    It shudders and absorbs the blow. The thunder
    crashes, laughing, applauding the toughness of the
    woodland king.
The fogs roll in on cats' paws from the sea,
  hiding the high limbs from the ground.
  The myriad needles blades transform the mist
    into minute particles which fall as gentle dew
    from heaven.

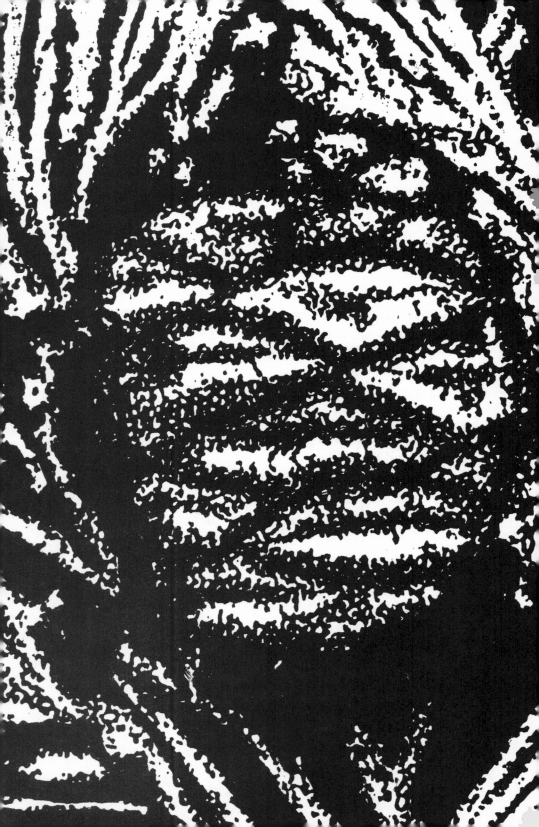

During the driest summer, the fog still visits nearly
every night.
  The dew falls. A mesh of thirsty fibers,
    greedily drinks the nectar from the sky.
A lightning fire or a blaze set thoughtlessly, rages through
the woods.
  Most living things are utterly destroyed;
The redwood's armored bark shields the heartwood.
The forest monarchs stand unscathed;
    the littered floor swept fire clean, they flourish.
  What are the steps by which those puny seeds are
changed
      into tough, living, ancient monuments,
        reaching to these towering heights?

HUMAN
SEED

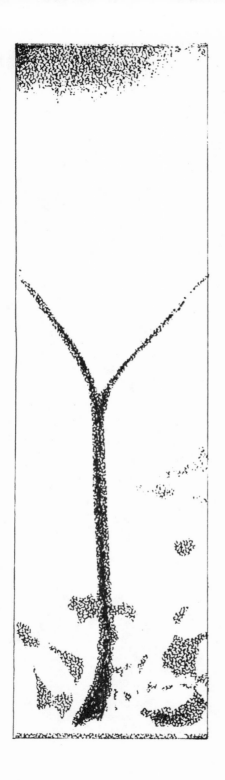

In my arms I cradle a newborn child, naked, helpless, crying
savagely.
No wonder it should rage, cast from the warmth and
nurture of the womb,
into an alien, cold and hostile world,
dependent now on fickle human love for warmth and
care,
if it is to survive at all.
How many years that baby seed needs nourishment and
gentle tending,
to grow to maturity, true humanness.
Emotionally and spiritually human children are like
baby kangaroos,
but only love, freely given, can provide their
pouch.

How fragile are these human seeds, spiritual embryos.
　　Many fail to reach full humanness.
　　　A fall, neglect, too much or little heat,
　　　　an unknown virus or some germ or lack of
　　　　love
　　　　and they are damaged beyond recognition or
　　　　destroyed.
　　And even those surviving into adulthood and maturity,
　　　only a few of them achieve fulfillment.

Then I think of the human giants, tall, soaring human
souls,
　　who have broken free of limitations.
　　They stand in two worlds, one foot based on earth
　　　among the rocks and plants and other human
　　　beings,
　　　the other grounded in eternity,
　　　at home in the vaster and more complicated world
　　　of spirits, good and evil, and of God.

A bright and shining cloud of witnesses passes before my
inner eye.
> These have moved from seedhood into their potent
> wholeness;
>> they have been touched by heaven.
There Buddha sits transfixed beneath his Bo tree,
> Confucius brings order to an Emperor's court,
> Laocius points to the way, the Tao.
> Mohammed brings virtue to a chaotic world.
And then I see Francis of Assisi with Lady Poverty,
 Catherine of Genoa ministering to the condemned and sick,
 Mark and Peter, Luke and John; and from out of the mists
 of memory
> the luminous figures of Abraham, Moses, Elijah and
> Isaiah.
And then Mother Julian appears and Ambrose and in their
company
 I perceive Plato and Augustine, Thomas of Aquinas and
 Athanasius.
They emerge unrelated to the time they lived,
> as time no longer holds them fast.
Another group comes into sight, Jung and Einstein,
 Shakespeare who knew God and Dante who sang
> of heaven, purgatory and of hell, earnest and with wit,
 Charles Williams and Eliot carried by wings of fancy to
> Paradise.
Personal figures emerge, my mother and father who have
fallen,
> so many friends, young and old, Cathy who died so young,
> Ruth and Shirley, John and Chuck.
> Ken cut down so suddenly, my brother,
> the grandparents whom I never knew.

And then I look around me at those now living,
    wife and friends still growing, who still withstand
    the storms and fires, earthquakes and floods,
        and reach relentlessly toward life eternal.

But suddenly my eye is caught and held:

    the most radiant light of all,
    the light from which all other lights are lit.
    I catch my breath. It is the Nazarene, Jesus the
    Christ.
    Here is the tree which reaches straight to heaven,
        the very axis of the world.
Beneath this central figure, the other hallowed humans
stand,
        reflecting this central light.
    They know the depth of rich earth and the reach of
heaven,
        their growth has never ceased.
    Gardens are planted around their roots.
        Nearby a lake reflects their glory, a brook plays
about their feet.
What has enabled them to scale such heights, attain such
size?

I see the wailing, naked infant, the frightened child, con-
fused teenager....
    And then consider these established ones who
    demonstrate,
    the depth and height and width and breadth we can
    attain.
What has enabled them to reach this consummation?
    What nurtured this fusion, earth and spirit merging?
How can we, you and I, unite the beast and angel in each of us?
How can we flourish like giant redwoods?

An answer came to me in the redwood's awesome mystery of
unflagging growth.
   The tree revealed the process of incredible increase.
   Within the dimness of the grove I meditate
 upon the grandeur of the trees;
And I discern the steps by which the redwood becomes a
giant,
a key was given which also unlocked the secret of our human
capacity
     for resurrected life.
I saw that human maturity and growth
     follow the more transparent pattern of the
     redwood tree.
   The amazing vitality of this giant plant offered me
   a ten-strand thread leading me through the
     labyrinth
       of human possibilities
       to its divine destiny.

THREAD OF
MANY STRANDS

— 3 —

Monarch of the forest, this colossus still requires
precise conditions to attain its majestic height and
age.
    Entering many times into the silent vastness of these
    groves,
        listening to my imagination and my heart, I
        found
    ten elements from which their gigantic bulk is
    built.
The first requirement is healthy seed, maturing in its cone
    and carried by the wind to some propitious spot.
    What marvelous wisdom this germ of life contains!
Yet if this embryo of life is incomplete
    defective or flawed, no tree is born.
When seeds are torn or bruised or cracked
    by bird or stone or falling limb,
        no mighty trees are born.

This germ of life remains forever potential only,
  until it soaks up water
 from earth or sky, from rivulet or rain.
    What activity and wisdom the moist spark ignites.
 It germinates. Root and trunk and leaf begin to grow.
Without this elixir, the seed does perish
 and so it cannot live.
 This sprouting plant, new and tender, sprouting, needs
both
earth and sky
 to spur its growth.

An environment of soft, moist earth
and pure rich air are vital to its life.
What a treasure house the dirt which cradles it,
composed of many elements: iron, manganese, zinc,
copper
and many others which the damp sets free.
The seedling requires traces of these many
minerals.
How many particles the invisible air contains,
ingredients the needle-like leaves drink in
and transform into living building blocks.
Landing on a rock or in an airless place,
the seed may germinate, but then it dies.

Like any plant, the tender sequoia shoot needs light.
　Without life-giving rays of sun, the seedling
　soon exhausts
　its inner store of energy;
　　it withers and expires.
The green stuff of the needle, leaf or algae, is a
chemical plant
　waiting for the sun and its particles of light to
　start and carry on
　the alchemy that transforms: air and water,
　minerals and sunlight,
　　into limbs and roots, bark and transforming
　　chlorophyll,
　Without the sun and its radiant gift
　　no plant would live; no animals survive.

And then the tree needs warmth to live and thrive, to rise.
The climate it requires is mild, the warmth of sun,
mild ocean breeze,
a warm seafog blanket, the fellowship of other
trees,
standing tall in unprotected groves.
Severe winters retard the sapling.
Frozen it may stand lifeless or split apart and perish.
With no warmth there is no life at all.

Time, time, and more time is the next ingredient.
   How much time these giants demand for full maturity.
     They are young when sycamores are aged and
     rotting,
       barely adult when oaks begin to fail
       after three hundred summers.
     Some were living when Jesus lay in his manger.
     The tree cries out: "Give me time. Time is sacred.
       Time alone brings forth my destiny."
Without slow flowing time no towering groves of
redwood
     or soaring human souls.

Day and night these trees work silently, unceasingly.
By day they seize the sun's particles of light.
  At night the work goes on, synthesizing compounds,
  producing different kinds of cells,
     preparing for another day of capturing the
     light.
  Roots drink in earth's nutrients.
   Pumps within the sapwood lift elements
    required by factories of green chlorophyll.
Always growth: building, healing wounds, preparing
buttresses.
   Growth goes on relentlessly, celebrating
discipline.

When saws lay bare the deep red heartwood of a fallen
monarch,
  there written in its own iconography is its history,
   chronicled year by year in concentric rings,
   a thousand, fifteen hundred years or more.
Every drought, fire, flood or lightning stroke is
recorded there.
  Written in its heartwood is its life.
How do these trees flourish when others perish?
  They protect themselves from nearly every foe.
   They erect defenses, and keep their fences mended.
    Insects and grubs will not touch the bark
     nor the heartwood saturated with chemicals
     insects cannot abide.
  Fires blazing through woodland groves burn myrtle,
oak and pine;

these great plants shudder, but thick bark
resistent to fire,
like asbestos, withstands the raging flames.
Even the heartwood is drenched in the very
tannic acid
    used in fire extinguishers to retard
    a fire.

What indomitable will to life these trees display,
    a kind of courage and persistence.
When ax or falling neighbor, avalanche or storm,
    strike the redwoods down, they rise phoenix-like.
    From stumps or fallen logs, new trees arise,
    become gigantic.
    These reborn trees in time may fall,
        only to live again.
    The same tree lives on and on,
        as immortal as any living thing.

How wise these mighty giants are, sequoia sempervirens,
   They provide ten clues to full growth now
      and in eternal life beyond:
      a healthy seed and dew from heaven,
      an environment of earth and air, sunlight and
      warmth,
      the work of many disciplines, the constant
      record of its life,
      relentless time, courage and persistence,
      and then resurrecting power.
These elements combine to fashion awesome groves of
kingly trees.
The same components give rise to human titans too.
   Each element has a story of its own to tell,
   reveals a portion of the way, the truth, the life.

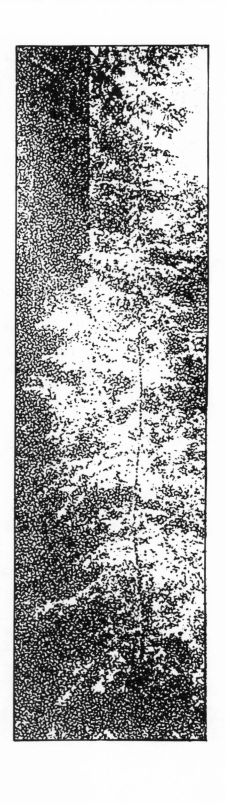

— 4 —

Upon my hand that redwood seed still lies. Like any seed
it is a mystery.

It is the gift of life, the bearer of immortality.

What hidden wisdom the seed contains.

Secrets innumerable are locked within its lifeless
husk,

mysteries it will reveal only when the time is
ripe and full,

infinite knowledge in a tiny grain of life.

When this potential life awakens a dozen miracles happen
all at once:

roots reach down to suckle earth,

water and food begin to move within its veins.

The roots spread out, laying foundations for its future
height.

A tiny shoot, a trunk in miniature, reaches up to drink in
air,

strains towards the sun.

Needles on delicate sprigs throw off the husk in which they
were conceived,
    green and powerful they offer leafage to the sun,
    ready to transmute particles of sunlight
        into energy and wood and bark and even cones
        and further seeds.
 These tender, newborn redwood needles are nothing less
    than miniscule, safe, efficient, complex factories,
creating building blocks of chemicals and cells,
    everything needed, required for a giant tree.
Chemical transformation start up, reactions so complex
    the best of human minds only now begin
    to unravel them, using all the knowledge of
    subatomic physics and organic chemistry.
Within the seed there is a blueprint
    for bark and root, sapwood, heartwood,
    burls and twigs, and sap and leaves.
The seed knows the seasons and provides cones with ripe
seeds,
    at times the earth is best prepared to nurture them.
Each seed knows its own destiny.
    An acorn conceives an oak, a peach pit creates
 a peach,
        This naked seed lying on my hand contains a giant
        redwood.
What incredible wisdom this germ of life contains,
apparently dried and dead,

This pod can wait for centuries to release its hidden
life,
    its marvelous, uncanny wisdom.
The power and perfection of this seed is more than I can
grasp,
    but how infinitely more astounding and complex
        that naked crying, newborn child;
    its body made up of many trillion cells,
    each knowing its own function and seldom going wrong,
    a brain making the most intricate computer
        look very simple;
    a million miles of roads and wires
        for transportation and communication,
    and containing the strange capacity of reproducing
        other creatures like itself.
Skin and bones, flesh, lungs and heart and glands,
    fearfully and wonderfully made this screaming child,
    All this contained first in an egg, fertilized and
nurtured in a womb
    and then brought forth as a wailing, helpless
child.
The infant then grows
    in mind, in body, and social sense,
    playing with others like itself.

Like wallabies human children must be nurtured in a
pouch,
   but the protection they require is not physical alone,
   but a psychic one as well created by the social web
      of family and friends, other children and those
      who teach,
      but most of all by loving, caring, self-giving
      love
         of dedicated parents.
Infants denied tender affection, fond touch and care
     often waste away and die. Marasmus, the deadly
    disease is called,
     that strikes babies who know no human touch.
Within this social incubator they learn to speak some
tongue,
   they learn to read and write and think,
        to tap the wisdom of the past.
     Becoming independent they cherish freedom,
     become adult.
     Creativity and imagination are expressed
     in thought and word, through hands and voice. They
learn to care, to love, to heal.
     Conscious and self-conscious they begin
     to wonder.

A great mutation can then occur, a transformation,
   The inner eye is opened and they perceive a new
   dimension
      beyond space and time and sense and earth.
      They can then discover that they are living souls,
         citizens of two intermingling worlds.
         They can participate in a vast spiritual realm.
         They do not die when bodies rot away.
      From launching pads of mortality and earth
         they streak out into the heavens,
            on quests eternal, never ending.

The human seed requires at least four births before
  this unique journey is begun.
  Human beings must be deeply grounded in creation,
  in humanness, in love
    before their ego shells are cracked and they begin
    their climb.
We need a home, a port, to which we can return,
  where we are comfortable and safe,
    before we venture into this strange domain
    or we may lose our way and be destroyed.
Most human seeds are not ready for wild adventure
  until late teens or early adulthood;
    Some do not crack their husks till middle age
    or death.
What infinite patience is necessary, what wisdom and
vigilence,
    if these human levels of maturing are to follow
    one another.
      The plant or human, when forced, is usually
      deformed.
How crucial for those bringing forth the seed to tend it
  until it is ready for another stage of growth.
I lead others best upon their journey as I stick
relentlessly to mine.
    And this incredible destiny is all contained
    potentially
in egg and sperm, in helpless childhood and youthful
rebellion.
How wonderful our nature is when we perceive
  our inner intricacy, our plan, our goal.

Some human seeds have been so damaged,
    by flaws within the germ of life or in
    womb's nurturing,
    or by lack of love, or caring,
    by hatred, neglect and cruelty,
      they do not realize their latent
      possibilities.
They are damaged men and women;
    they must be protected to survive at all.
With earnest effort and love creating a new pouch,
    a few can be redeemed and start upon
    the interrupted journey.
What God intends, or now is doing, for these damaged
ones
    is hidden from our sight. We can provide compassion,
    for we might have shared their lot.
But the one who lets no sparrow fall unnoticed,
has a destiny for them as well.
    We do not see, we cannot know, what prayer
      and tender love and Eucharist are working
      in their depth.

SEED AND EGO

— 5 —

Germination is a strange process. It contains both death
and life;
    like a new year, the old is cast aside, the new
    begins.
The static perfection of the seed is thrown out of
balance, undermined.
    Water seeps through husk and miracles occur.
      In arid Arizona after long wet winters
        the earth comes suddenly to life,
        and the desert blossoms.
      Seeds lying there dormant for many years
      waken to life
        laying purple blankets over vast
        slopes
        and painting hills with red and
        orange.

Grain unearthed in dry Egyptian tombs,
planted in moist soil begin to
swell and sprout.
(Some tiny, primitive animals can be
quickly dried,
sleep quietly like seeds,
and stir to life and movement when touched
with a drop of water.)
From the seeds' constricted point of view,
germinating is not a pleasant process.
Penetrating through the shell, the water
stirs activity.
The germ of life is quickened, swells,
begins to *live*.
The husk, the pod, the shell are no longer large
enough.
Compressed, confined, expanding vitality
cracks the husk.
Its protection splits apart, a rootlet and
a shoot appear,
entering a strange and sometimes
hostile world.
These new beings must expand or die,
face drought and flood, animal and bird,
and overshading trees to obtain security
as lofty mature sequoia.
Gone is the closed finality of seedhood.

Human birth is difficult at best,
    from the mother's or the baby's frame of reference.
The environment was perfect. The unborn child was
nourished,
    warmed, protected, carried, cleansed.
Now it is expelled from paradise, pushed, thrust, pommeled
    and cast into an alien world, totally dependent and
    helpless.
        And still it must burst out or die.
Emerging from the womb is the child's second birth.
 The first was in the mating of the sperm and egg.
        Both died and something new began.
    It has two more husks to crack, discard.
The growing child must learn the joy of bonding
    and of dependency, being held and touched and
    loved.

And no sooner is total reliance, trust established
   and it too gives way. The child cries out:
      "Mother, let me do it for myself."

The adolescents mature into egohood, assured, secure,
   capable of dealing with school, with friends and
   bullies, with the other sex,
   with cars, exams, with work, rejection and even
marriage
      striking out as independent individuals,
      these confident
         new men and women start new families
         and nurture them.

But even this adaptation becomes restrictive, a confining
alley leading nowhere.
   A hankering for they-know-not-what plagues them like
   an itch.
   They must escape or stagnate, must be born once more,
      through a dark passageway into an even stranger
      world.
Telling his own tale, Jung describes this encounter
   with unknown, spiritual reality as great blocks of
   stone falling down upon him.
St. John, the Spanish poet and follower of the cross, describes the dark night
   which begins in the quiet of one's house
and brings one to the Divine Lover's embrace
while the breeze whispers among the turrets of the Castle.
The apostle Paul cries out: "That which you sow
   cannot come to life except it die;
   There are also celestial bodies and bodies terrestial."
Into an unfathomable abyss we are born again.
Within the dark we move slowly toward the light.
 We slip back and then we start our journey once again.

The water which sparks this final and unending stage
of birthing
    is our humbling human need, our desire for more
    than we can dream of or achieve by our own effort,
        the pain and hurt of purely human dead-end
        streets.
    The inner swelling and the suffering begin again.
Into the dazzling darkness we emerge as the husk cracks
open,
 and new pathways are needed, new directions, new maps.
        Usually the road is steep and narrow,
        difficult.

    We die daily and rise again. With each step
    we venture
        further into a strange new world,
        inexhaustible
        in depth and mystery; it is so easy
        to lose one's way.

Sometimes these births seem like inner crucifixions.
    I remember the words of one who was
    crucified
    outwardly as well as inwardly:
    "Pick up your cross and follow me."
How many times I find I must be born again.
    Unless I lose my life I do not find it.
    Sometimes I get very tired of all
    this growth.
        New vistas demand new adaptations,
        and I get sick of change and
        transformation.

This is no easy way, this multiple fourth birth.
　There is no turning back.
　The plant cannot retreat and be a seed again.
　Nor can we return to innocence
　　once the membrane which protects us has
　　split apart.
　Once we are thrust out of Eden
　　into the limitless spiritual world of which
　　we are a part,
　　where good and evil, angels and demons are
　　contending,
　　　there is no forgetting, no oblivion,
　　　except madness.
　We are open now, defenseless, unprotected.
　　The universe is larger than our wildest dream,
　　extending far beyond the furthest star.
　　We need a guide to find our way.

One telling difference separates the redwood seed
    and the human spiritual embryo.
      When water seeps through its shell,
      then a tiny sequoia breaks forth. It has
      no choice.
    You and I can refuse this final birthing process.
      We can set our feet against it and remain
      a stone.
When living things refuse to germinate,
 and the proper time for growth has come,
 death, agony, or disaster usually takes place.
The ovum unfertilized is sloughed away;
   The infant remaining in the womb soon dies.
    The child afraid to enter adulthood
    is childish and half human.
Adults rejecting cosmic birth condemn themselves,
   (they are not condemned) to meaningless
   existence,
   sterility and fear, to neurosis and confusion.
Confronted by death they have no hope.
   They survive with denial, anger, bitterness
   and fear,
    at best with stoic calm.
   They have rejected the opportunity to know the new life
   that cosmic birth reveals.
    And this is hell.

Some people think it is their duty to crack the husks of
others.
   They see the danger and the potential of human destiny,
   and anxiously they take control and dominate.
      Some religious orders have created conditions
         to force the soul to open up.
      Some fearful bigots in religion's name
      use fear, pressure, judgment, power
         to force the soul to break its bounds
         and grow.
Some play with cosmic birth as if it were a game.
 They swallow drugs and flirt with psychic powers
 and people blow apart.
God alone knows how and when to discard the ego husk,
   preparing for further births and transformations.
   The eternal knows all secrets of the heart
      and demands no more than we can bear.
   When human beings take over God's prerogative,
      they are cruel or stupid, or demonic.
   When plants are forced to grow they are injured
   and deformed;
      The same is true of animals and human souls.

What can we do to help a soul trapped in its sheath?
We can suffer with them, have compassion and
bear with them
with love, and caring, listening and
patient prayer.
Pray, pray, remembering that only God
gives this kind of birth,
and sometimes gives it secretly.
Judging people caught in unbirth seldom remove the
blocks,
and often makes birth impossible for them.
Compassion, love and prayer are the best midwives
into rebirth and life eternal.

These births occur in two quite different ways.
One occurs silently, often unobserved.
Nurtured from childhood into an
expanded universe,
Many are drawn gently towards renewal and
rebirth
by dogma and sacrament. By daily
inward turning,
Eucharist, reflection, listening
they find rebirth.
They are gently melted, molded, used;
understanding and experience increase
bit by bit.
The poor often receive their transformation quietly
for they are already torn open by adversity.
God loves the poor and the poor in spirit.
Hunger, poverty and grief can melt away the shell.

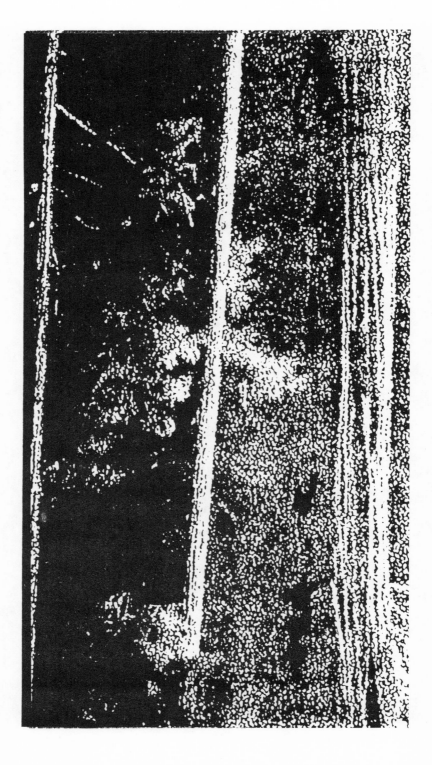

The other birth is more striking and dramatic.
   The rich, the wise, the charming and intelligent
   are often imprisoned in time and space,
   in their own wills and power.
   To them this world and what it holds alone is real
   and they will have their part of it.
      They reject any possibility of something more
      than what they know and can control.
It takes a cataclysm to penetrate their pit-like seed.
   Suddenly a light appears, a voice, a blindness
   as to Paul on the Damascus road.
   Often they are convulsed and agonized,
      the birth is full of torment and of anguish.
      This may take place at death or even later.
   Suddenly they see, their lives are totally reversed,
   their values overturned; they are transformed.
   Many of the leaders of the faith have had such births,
   St. Augustine, St. Francis, John Newton of
Amazing Grace,
      and many, many others.
      They know. They speak with authority and power.
      Theirs is the only way.
      Sometimes they scorn the way of gradual
      regeneration.

There are two ways of passage to rebirth.
   They need each other as brother and sister,
      respecting and understanding one
      another.
   The important matter is not the process but the birth,
      the spiritual germination.

EARTH,
AIR,
AND WATER
OF THE SOUL

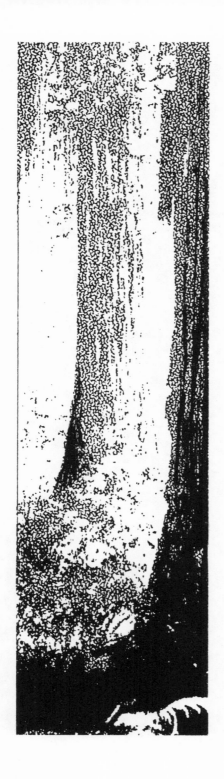

— 6 —

How careless we have been of this fragile earth,
our island home.
  We now know that earth and sky, stream and sea
  live in very delicate balance with one another.
    Polluted waters poison all living things.
    The earth is raped, destroyed, left desolate,
      and only barren rocks remain.
    Contaminated air can change the climate
      and its wind become a scourge.
  Most plants require a special kind of place:
    palms do not grow on alpine slopes
    nor spruce in marshes by the sea.
There was a time when redwoods covered much of the
primeval land
  but earth has changed and is no longer kind to them
    except in a few unique localities where their
    needs are met.

The park-like groves of giant trees love
   well-watered, sandy river valleys, with
   misty mornings
   bright, warm, brilliant afternoons
   and mild night fogs protecting them from cold.

The redwood seed may germinate on blotting paper or in a
vacuum,
   but it will live only a few days without earth and
   air.
The tiny newborn roots need rich, moist earth
   where they can burrow and seek the atoms with which
   they build.
They drink in water and the elements,
   starting a process and progression towards immensity.
      Water is necessary for all organic life.
      The redwood magically transforms this fluid
      into trunk and leaves
         and it becomes the essence of its blood-like
         sap.

We are just beginning to understand the rich complexity
   of common dirt and the many different elements
   within it that life requires.
      We human animals can starve when fed on plants,
         grown in impoverished, or depleted soil.
      We need traces of many different elements
         or we are ill and weak.
The redwood has similar requirements: a bit of iron,
   a trace of copper, phosphorus, manganese and zinc,
      to mention but a few.
Some are built into the structure of the tree,
  while others stimulate involved chemical processes
     as catalysts.
Other earthy elements – sulphur, mercury or lead – can
sterilize
    the earth and render her quite barren.
Too much of any element can destroy the balance.
   Ancient cities, sown with salt by angry
   conquerors,
      remain deserts to this day.

Unless the milieu of the earth contains a pharmacy of
chemicals
   and in the right proportion, development is stunted
      or the vital flame goes out.
      Near the great trees are pygmy forests.
      The soil is alkaline and so retards these plants
         that trees, a hundred years of age,
         are no bigger than my thumb.
   Different segments of the trees have different
   resquisites.
The needles need one combination of elements to do their
work,
   the sap still others, the bark must have its red tannic
   acid,
   and the solid heartwood trunk needs carbon in great
   abundance.
The tree takes naked elements into itself
   and creates an ancient living giant.

The soil, however, important as it is, is not enough.
    The tree needs air as well.
    The leaves or needles breathe in the atmosphere
        and incorporate invisible particles into
        the rising living wooden column.
    Swaying in the breeze the needles comb the sky,
        absorbing the very substances in which they
        dance.
Oxygen and nitrogen are plentiful.
    Many other gases are found in small amounts,
    But it is carbon gas, carbon dioxide,
        only a tiny fraction of the air,
        a substance we cannot even see,
    which is essential for every plant and shrub and tree.
    The redwood works miracles with this gas.
First the tree breaks down this carbonic-acid gas
    and combines the carbon with water
    to build its trunk and roots, its twigs and needles,
    its sap and bark.
        All organic stuff has this beginning,
            the very matter which has softened earth's crust
                creating a home for all of us.

During the process of transformation the
chemical-factory-needles
    release life-giving oxygen into the atmosphere.
Through millions of years the cloak of air around the
earth
    has been transformed through silent working
    of redwoods and all other plants.
Vegetation has created conditions so animals can
walk upon the earth
    and birds can soar into the sky.
These kindly plants have made the world our island
home.

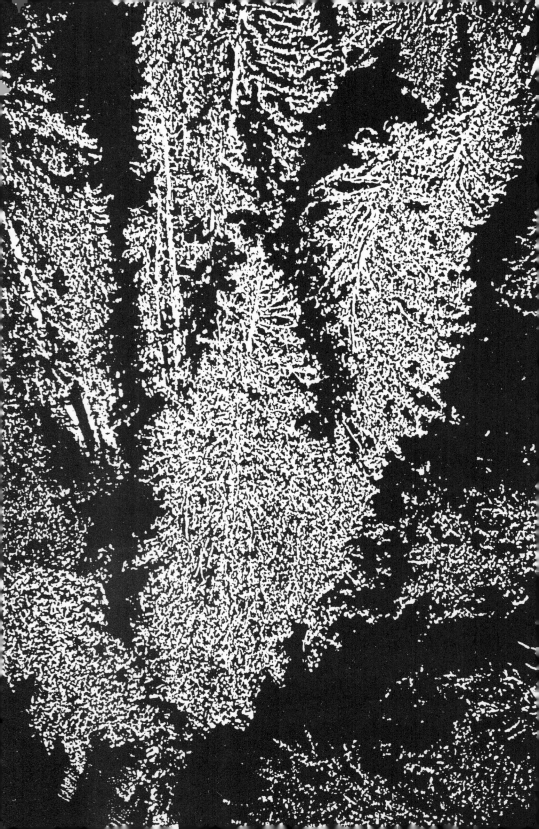

The newborn baby requires an environment so complex
   that only other human beings can create it.
      In addition to the natural envelope of earth
      and sky and air and sun, it needs a biosphere.
      Abandoned infants soon are dead.
Young children, emerging from the womb, must be
nursed
      and clothed and warmed and changed.
      They must be fondled, touched and loved.
        Sung to, they learn to speak and sing.
        Played with, they learn to play.
        They respond to smiles, to laughter, tears;
          and slowly they become personalities.

They learn to deal with cold and snow and cliffs,
   and falling stones, with fire and cars,
   with parents and adults,
   with hostile children and with friends.
  Something more is locked within the growing child
   a thirst insatiable to learn and know,
   seeking to explore and understand and soak up
    all there is to see and do and find.
  Reading and writing reveal the treasury
    the past conceals, and gives into our hands
    its secrets, gems, its tragedy and gold.
Earth and sky and sociality do not exhaust
    the envelope of our environment.
  We cannot live by bread alone, the master said.
    Bread is a perfect symbol of the total world
    of matter
      and of the web our culture weaves,
      what earth has given and human hands have
      made.

We move within a world of spirit as well as in an earthy one.
  Another realm, a vast dimension surrounds us too,
  as real and hidden as the air the redwood breathes.
    We don't respond creatively to spirit
    unless we're taught that it is there
    and how to deal with the principalities
    and thrones
    with cosmic powers of dark and light.
  Our environment is partly intangible;
  we cannot cope with it without a vision of the
  world,
      an understanding and a plan of action
        which integrates this realm and earth.
  Unlike the redwood trees, we cannot, do not use
  this pneuma unless we're told it's there.

Primitives and natural people are more concerned with the spirits
    of this ethereal realm than
    with the stones and hills and animals around them.
And children also know this domain instinctively
    until adults condition them against it,
    hiding it from sight and use.
For several centuries we people of the West
have denied and laughed at
spirits, demons, elves and trolls.
    What they touched and heard and smelled and saw
    alone were real; all else illusion,
      the figment of wishful imagination.
    We are of the earth, earthy and that is all.

This deception has split us off from one whole realm of
fact.
　　We even forgot the necessity of love,
　　　　that touch and caring keep us alive
　　　　and heal the broken heart.
　　Few primitives have been so unnatural and deprived
　　as we who thought ourselves so rational and advanced.

　　How impossible to share in a universe
　　　　whose very existence we spurn and doubt.
　　We blind ourselves by our denial
　　　　and we do not perceive an entire realm of being.
　　　　　What we do not expect to see
　　　　　is often not discerned at all.
　　　　We become like trees deprived of air and wind
　　　　　and sky.
　　　　We're starved and a deep within cries out.
　　Neurosis is often the agony of trying to exist
　　　　without the air of spirit.

We human beings can deny any aspect of our environment,
    and live as though it were not real.
    The West has denied and so lost touch with spirit.
      But we can reject the earth, our bodies, even
      human love.
We can also deny the hard world of unyielding earth,
    our pain and hurts, our loneliness and grief,
    the agony of groaning existence;
      we can even still our heart crying in sympathy
      and try to live as pure spirit, unembodied.

Buddha refused to tolerate the scandal
    of our human misery.
    He searched until he found a discipline,
    a path that gave relief
      from pain, desire and blind will.
To bring his healing balm to human agony
    He journeyed through all of India
    until he died at eighty.
Much of the Orient has followed his way of wisdom.
    Many disillusioned Western men and women
    have turned East to find a path of hope;
    their lost heritage has failed
      to meet their need.
Less wise are those who will not face our anguish
    and give simplistic roads
      to hide from it.
Such mortals can become like trees
    floating rootless in the air.
Psychosis is living unconscious of the earth
    or of our bodies or of accepted rules
      if dealing with our common world.

But most of us are caught in a crassly material world.
    We seek to gain mastery, we struggle and strive
        to gain control; the stress and tension are
        incredible.
    And when success seems nearly in our grasp,
        then death or disaster strikes us from behind
        and we are powerless again, defeated.
    This relentless greed is but another form of madness.
        Imprisoned in earthy dungeons
      we cannot die to avarice and self-sufficiency.
We fail to take the last step of maturation.
    We do not die and then rise again, whole,
      born again in humble, wise maturity,
in a land larger than earth, kinder than home.

How can we recover our full universe—
all of its dimensions and its grandeur?
We need time to pause and wonder
to be still and listen to the breath of spirit.
 We need space to stop and ponder,
  quietly to wait upon another world.
  We can learn to think and question,
   become doubters of the conventional,
   of what most consider obvious.
The greatest modern men and women of science,
  are no longer certain of what they know.
   They do not understand what matter really
   is.
   And so they do not tell us what cannot be;
    they do not scoff at spirit and
    religion.
    Sometimes they are more open than theology
    to this reality.
Heisenberg, the greatest physicist of all,
put it well; he said that science has become so
skeptical
 it is even skeptical of its skepticism.
He also tells us that "God" and "Spirit" and "soul"
 are words more crammed full of meaning and
 experience and reality
 than the words of physics
  which have lost their former meaning.

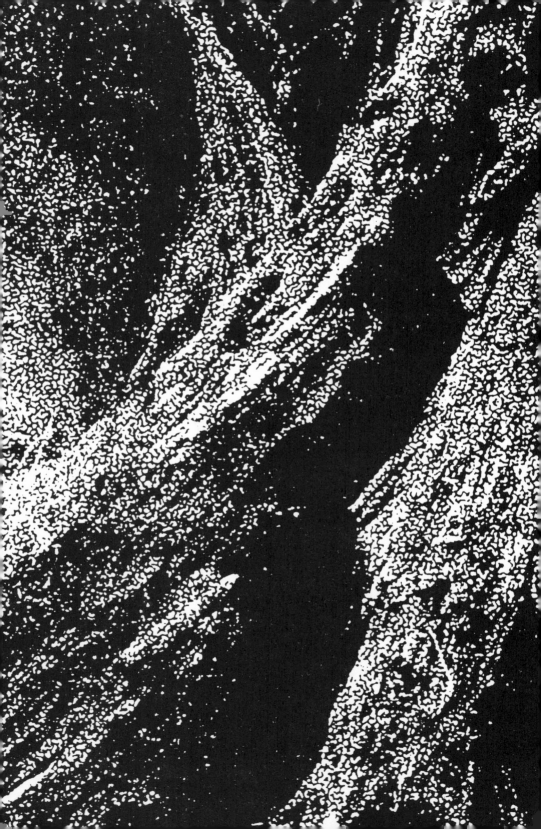

And then we can be still and hear
   the voices speak within and take account
   of visions presented to the inner eye.
   We can be saved from our worst fears and doubts.
     Renewal, hope and transformation are given as
     free gifts.
       And then we KNOW we are surrounded by
       angelic power
         as well as by materiality.
   We know this empowering mystery by our own encounter,
     not just from the tales of others.
The tree requires both earth and sky,
   or else it withers and then dies.
   Human beings need a larger universe;
     the world of earth and sea and sky and sun,
     the delicate fabric of human love and care,
     and the vast domain of spirit,
       of cherubim and seraphim and other powers.
   Unless we have all three we are like stunted trees,
     we are only partly human.

MIRACLE
OF LIGHT

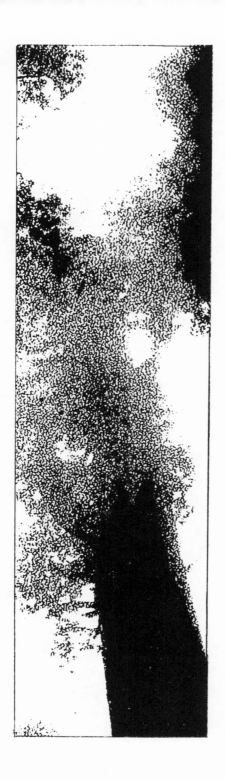

— 7 —

Light is a mystery defying human understanding;
   the wisest of most learned are still puzzled
   as they seek to grasp its essential nature.
      Light streaks through the endless corridors
      of space and time,
      moving with untiring feet, with never slackened
      pace.
No other moving object can match its dazzling speed.
      Without this light there is no clarity or sight,
      no warmth of plant or bird or animal.
The boiling furnace of the sun provides most of the
light
      which earth and its growing things receive.

Our sun, however, is but a tiny star
   compared to others which dot the firmament.
Some great stars explode and create new life.
   Light is the secret of creation and of life.
     The redwood which fails to seize its
     share of light
       becomes an ancient, whitened skeleton. . .
     Few grasses, ferns or shrubs survive
       in the dim, park-like, silent groves
       because the towering giants have
       absorbed the sun.

Equally mysterious are those green needles filled with
chlorophyll
    transforming this light into a living, growing tree,
       the miracle of photosynthesis.
   For many billion years the light and green have worked
       changing the barren volcanic rock and empty seas
       into our dear green earth and oceans
   teeming with myriad plants and fish, birds and
   creeping things.
The vital greenery of leaf and plant and needle,
      captures the particles of light, free electrons,
      and combines them with the other substances
      it stores.
         Carbohydrates are formed, the basic
         constituents
         of the whole organic realm of nature,
      simultaneously oxygen is freed, the atmosphere
      remade.

This redwood by its own alchemy has transmuted
     energy into form and substance.
     Lifting its verdant crown into the sky it caught the
     light
          and brought it down to be a part of earth:
               the wedding of mass and potency.
Most energy comes from the sun directly
     or indirectly the sun's rays are
          stored away through interminable ages
               in coal and peat, in oil and shale.
     Logs blazing, crackling in the stove or hearth
give forth
          the sun's light the trees have squirreled away.
     Nuclear reactors violently release this power
artificially
          which sun and stars provide so safely for us.
Some folk apparently wise and solemn,
     argue that these subtle and complex processes,
          so strangely intertwined and dependent
          on one another,
     arose from blind chance and bubbling mud pots.
     What do these doubters fear?
The savages rising early to greet the sun
     and falling down before some symbol of this
     flame
          in crude shrines of stone and clay,
     may be wiser than those who reverence nothing
     but themselves.

Today we are less dependent on the sun.
  We create light and warmth using the refuse
  that trees and plants and creatures of the sea
  have left behind.
  We think ourselves quite self-sufficient
    and forget our dependence on the light.
  How easily forgotten is the more important,
  inner light,
  from those whose image the sun and stars were struck.

Until we mortal men and women are exposed
   to this inner light and absorb it into ourselves,
We are not born again.
   We fail to realize our final maturation.
   Our destiny, human and divine, is not fulfilled.
Without this inner sun, without its blaze,
   the vast, inner, psychic realm is dark and haunted.
   Dark monsters of the deep lurk and prowl,
      seeking whom they may devour;
Only the bravest heroes dare venture there.
      At times the outer world is dim and
      threatening as well.
      When both worlds are devoid of light,
         we are torn apart within a deep abyss of
         blind chaos.

The light divine has always blazed and millions have been
blessed
by its radiant glow, its warmth, its vital energy.
    Unlike the tree upon which the light falls or not,
        (there is nothing a tree can do but crowd the
        others out),
    we living souls can either seek the light or hide
    from it.
        The holy flame is real, and unyielding
        in its love.
        It forces us to further transformation.
    We can enclose ourselves in close-fitting
    metal spheres
        of busyness and ignorance.
    Or we can bare ourselves to this luminous sanctity,
        the soul's sustaining sun,
    and let its rays renew, change and transform us.
        It alone can vanquish the darkness,
        through the endless resurrections the
        spiritual world provides.

Mere words cannot convey the richness of this inner
brightness.
    Words fail to tell of all its grace and healing
love.
        But words also fall short in picturing our
human love
        and so we resort to song and poetry, to
        images.
How many seers of different times and faiths
        have praised this vital dazzling cloud of
peace
        and power and love and joy and strength.
        The best of every age have bared
themselves
        before the holy rays day after day
and so were built
        into substantial, whole, real human
        beings.
        They have become transparent creatures of earth
and light,
        shedding light and hope themselves.
        Imperceptibly they grow like trees
        whose roots are
            firmly planted in dirt and rock,
            whose trunk soars into eternity.

Waiting silently, attentive, within the luminous haze,
　a voice speaks softly calling us by name,
　guiding, directing, comforting.
　　Out of the brightness hands appear, then
　　arms,
　　a being of light to embrace and hold us fast,
to heal our hurts and wounds, redeem our lostness
and quench our thirst for love
that Love alone can satisfy.
　John of the Cross told of his meeting
　　in words better than I can frame:
　"This light guided me more surely than the light of
　noonday,
to the place where he (well I knew who!) was awaiting
　　me —
　　A place where none appeared....
Upon my flowery breast, kept wholly for himself
alone,
There he stayed sleeping, and I caressed him, the
fanning
　of the cedars made a breeze.
The breeze blew from the turret as I parted his
locks;
With his gentle hand he wounded my neck and caused
all my senses
　to be suspended.
I remained, lost in oblivion; My face I reclined on my
Beloved.
All ceased and I abandoned myself, leaving my cares
forgotten
　among the lilies."

Sometimes this image has been blurred and indistinct;
  We humans failed to comprehend the nature of that
  light.
    This eternal shekina wanted to be known as love as
    well as light.
The light became incarnate, took flesh, dwelt among us.
    The cosmic birth occurred preceded by a star.
    "...and that life was the light of men,
    a light that shines in the dark,
    a light that darkness could not overpower....
    The Word was the true light
    that enlightens all men;
    and he was coming into the world.
    He was in the world
    that had its being through him,
    and the world did not know him.
    He came into his own
    and his own people did not accept him.
    But to all who did accept him
    he gave power to become children of God.....
    Indeed, from his fullness we have, all of us,
    received——
    yes, grace in return for grace....*

*(JB-John 1:4,5,9-12,16)

Far more than gentle, healing, persevering good,
　this bright glory at the heart of things
　　has played the hero and the conqueror.
The light came into the murky darkness of our world,
　wrestled with blackness and was not overcome.
Love met proud evil, full of hate and scorn,
　The light was crucified and died.
　The prince of darkness and his host rejoiced,
　but their time of glee was short.
After three days light broke the inky bonds of death,
　and rose resplendent and victorious.
In dread the hosts of evil fled.
　　"The powers of death have done their worst,
　　But Christ their legions hath dispersed;
　　Let shout of holy joy outburst.
　　He closed the yawning gates of hell,
　　The bars from heaven's high portals fell;
　　Let hymns of praise his triumphs tell!"*
For reasons known to love divine alone,
　this creative sun reaches out to us,
　seeks to rescue us from darkness,
　　to ransom us from evil,
　　　to lift us from the pit
　　　　and share the victory
　　　　with all of us.
No power of hell or chaos, of bale or woe,
　No Satanic craft or wile
　has any final claim on you or me.
In hands of light the final reckoning lies.

(Hymn 91, Episcopal Hymnal, vs. 2, 4)

The tree has only day in which to drink the light.
    You and I can bask at any time in light divine,
    transforming mortality into eternal life.
        In dead of night, in silence and detached
        we often can perceive this brilliance best.
    Just as light creates new substances within the leaf,
        so the inner light conceives a new being
        within the soul,
        makes us children of Love itself,
        heirs to a kingdom now and forever,
        and frees us from the black abyss,
        defeats the dark forces that would
        drag us there.
    The source of light lays down but one requirement.
    Children of light must share the rays they have
    received,
        with family and friends, with alien and
        enemy.

The master said: "You are the light of the world....
Let your light so shine that all may see your good
works,
   and glorify your father in heaven."
When all of us will but expose our inner selves
   to spiritual photosynthesis,
the earth will be covered with the glory of God,
   as the water covers the sea.
And but a few baring their souls before the light,
   became the Christophers, light carriers, and
   changed our earth;
    Life sustaining light and love were then set free
     into the human fellowship
     as oxygen into the atmosphere.
    Earth might be fair and all its people free.

How can we bare ourselves before the light?
　We cannot find this transforming luminosity
　　until we have some idea that it's there
　　waiting to enlighten us.
　Someone reveals the light through word or deed
　　or we find a hint
　　in nature or in a book
　　and seek to find it for ourselves.
　　　Such rich and unfailing love is
　　　difficult for us
　　　to image since we have known so
　　　little from so few.
And then we stop our busyness, cease our striving.
　We turn inward seeking for what we hope to find.
　　In silence and detachment, passive for the
　　moment,
　　our awareness widens; deepens and we perceive
　　a larger range of knowing
　　　which ordinary occupation with the
　　　earth
　　　and with survival have shut out.

Into this new world we step with phantasy
   (a world which dreams and ancient myths
   have intimated and revealed).
We invoke the light; it appears, gradually
at times,
and sometimes like a flash of lightning.
   What patience is required of some of us
   who are accustomed to direct and rule.
Slowly the transformation begins within,
   imperceptibly the kingdom of heaven
   grows,
      within us on earth as it will
      be in heaven.

The light appears in many other ways as well,
   in Eucharist and ritual, in loving
   relationship,
watching children play, in music and great
art,
   as death approaches, sometimes in pain
   and suffering,
   often in dreams and ecstasy.
The light is more present than we often realize,
   seeking us and reaching out relentlessly.
The inner journey can be a dangerous
undertaking,
   unless we have a guide, a light, an inner
   friend.
   Beware of flattering imitations, inferior
   spirits.
      Why settle for a lesser guide when
      Christ himself,
      the way, the truth and life
      will come and lead us through the
      maze?
We are so easily deceived.
   We also need the human comradeship and warmth
   of fellow searchers, stalkers of the light.
   They help us bear the darkness
   and guide us toward the light.